Going Places

Ellen Lawrence

LIGHTBOX
openlightbox.com

Go to **www.openlightbox.com** and enter this book's unique code.

ACCESS CODE

LBL29588

Lightbox is an all-inclusive digital solution for the teaching and learning of curriculum topics in an original, groundbreaking way. Lightbox is based on National Curriculum Standards.

OPTIMIZED FOR

- ✓ TABLETS
- ✓ WHITEBOARDS
- ✓ COMPUTERS
- ✓ AND MUCH MORE!

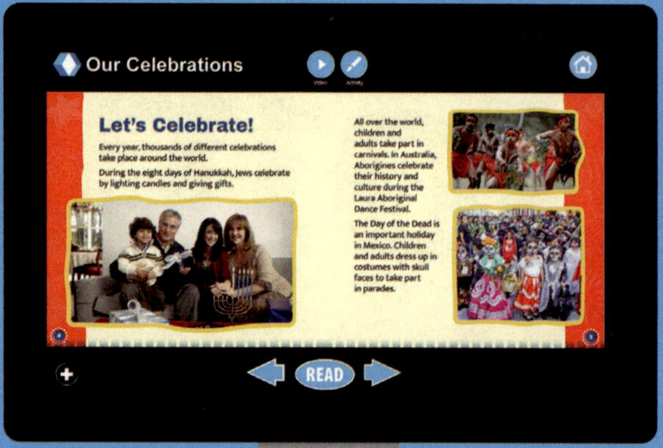

STANDARD FEATURES OF LIGHTBOX

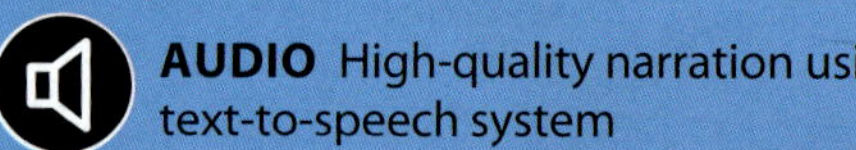
AUDIO High-quality narration using text-to-speech system

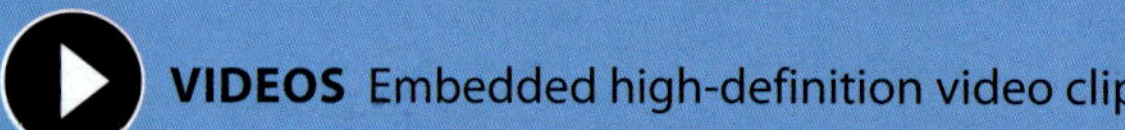
VIDEOS Embedded high-definition video clips

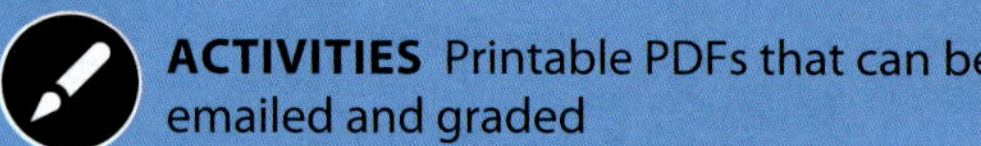
ACTIVITIES Printable PDFs that can be emailed and graded

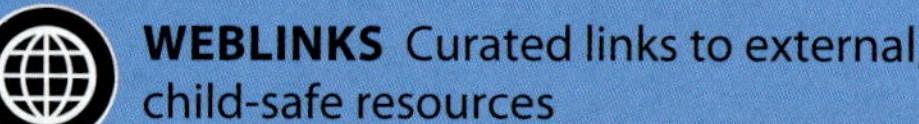
WEBLINKS Curated links to external, child-safe resources

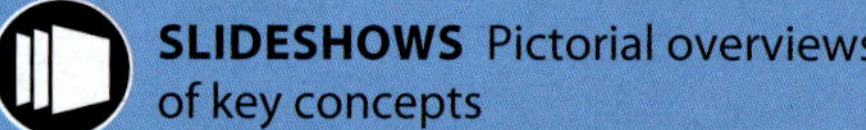
SLIDESHOWS Pictorial overviews of key concepts

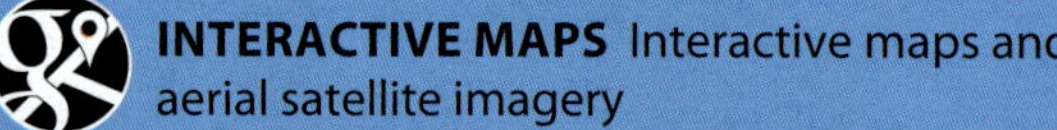
INTERACTIVE MAPS Interactive maps and aerial satellite imagery

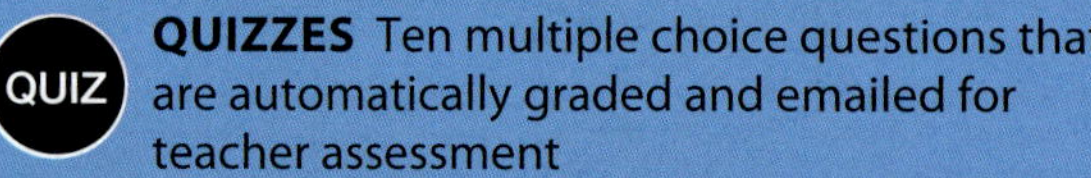
QUIZZES Ten multiple choice questions that are automatically graded and emailed for teacher assessment

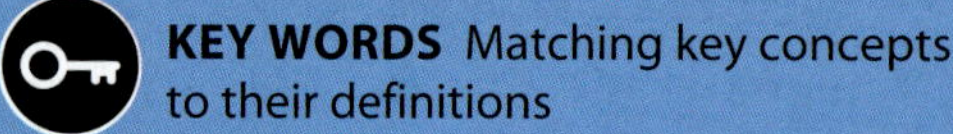
KEY WORDS Matching key concepts to their definitions

VIDEOS

WEBLINKS

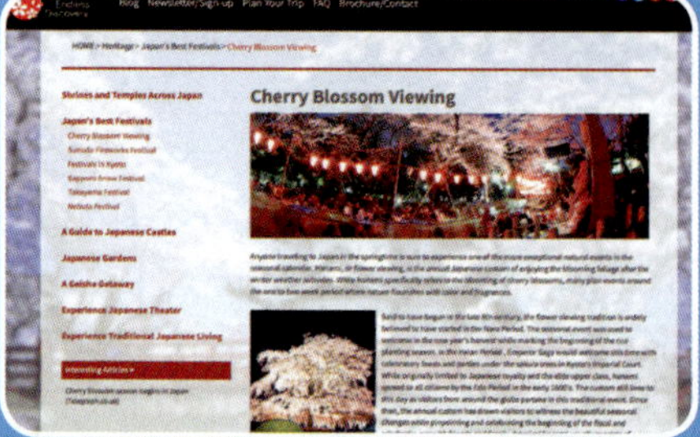

SLIDESHOWS

QUIZZES

About Our World

Going Places

How Do We Get Around?

Every day, people are on the move.

In cities, some people drive small electric cars. When these cars are parked, they can be plugged in and recharged.

People and goods are sometimes carried by oxcarts in Myanmar. In snowy Mongolia, herders travel by reindeer. Entire families in Colombia will pack onto a single motorbike.

In Guatemala, many people travel by bus. These buses once took kids to school in the United States. Now they travel from village to village in their new home. Their yellow paint is replaced with colorful new looks.

All Aboard the School Bus

From Monday to Friday, yellow school buses can be seen on roads across the United States and Canada.

Each morning, about 30 million children climb aboard these yellow buses. It takes 500,000 buses and drivers to get that many kids to school every day!

The bright yellow color of school buses was chosen because it can easily be seen. Making school buses easy to see helps keep children safe.

The oldest school bus in the United States is at the Henry Ford Museum in Dearborn, Michigan.

A Pedal Power School Bus

On the crowded streets of Delhi in India, many people travel in rickshaws. These small carriages are pulled by a driver on foot or riding a bicycle. Many children travel to school in rickshaws.

The drivers have to weave in and out of the cars, vans, people, and other rickshaws on the crowded streets.

For many kids, the journey to school can take two hours!

Off to School by Canoe

Every morning in Nigeria, small canoes filled with school children set off across a lagoon. The lagoon is near Lagos, which is Nigeria's biggest city.

The children live in fishing villages on one side of the lagoon. Their school is on the other side of the lagoon. The older kids paddle the canoes, while their younger friends enjoy the ride to school.

The children travel to school in the canoes that their fathers use for fishing. After school, the children paddle home. Then their fathers use the canoes again to go fishing.

Animal Power

From camels to horses, dogs, and donkeys, animals help humans get around.

People have traveled by horse and donkey power for about 5,000 years. Horses and donkeys were originally wild animals. Over time, our ancestors tamed and trained them.

In Greenland, Inuit people have traveled by dog sled for thousands of years. Each dog in a team can pull one and a half times its own weight over snow and ice. The sled dogs are tough, powerful animals that enjoy working for their owners.

Snowmobiles

In many snowy places around the world, dog sleds have been replaced by snowmobiles. A snowmobile is a sled that's powered by an engine.

In Norway, Sami reindeer herders live alongside their animals.

The large herds of reindeer move from place to place to find food. As the animals walk over the icy, snowy land, the herders ride alongside on snowmobiles.

Sami people call themselves "reindeer walkers." That's because they used to walk or ski for hundreds of miles alongside their reindeer herds.

Taking the Train

Traveling by train is one way to get around.

Trains in many countries around the world can be crowded with people traveling to see their families on a holiday.

In China, people get to ride on the fastest train in the world. The maglev train in the city of Shanghai reaches a top speed of 268 miles per hour (431 km/h).

Passengers can watch how fast they are going on screens in the carriages.

The longest passenger train in the world is in Australia. It is almost 0.75 miles (1.2 km) long.

Flying Doctors

Most people are used to visiting the doctor if they are sick. In an emergency, they might take an ambulance to the hospital. In the outback of Australia, it's not always that simple.

Many people in the outback live hundreds of miles from a doctor or hospital. So when people need help, doctors come to them by plane.

A flying doctor might actually have to operate on a patient inside the plane. Sometimes the plane acts like a flying ambulance and carries a patient to the nearest hospital.

Walking All the Way

From cars to bikes, buses to trains, and rickshaws to canoes, there are many ways to travel to school. There's one way, however, that kids use all over the world—their feet!

Schoolchildren in South Africa walk to school. Sometimes they bring chairs from their homes with them.

Many children in Great Britain get to school by traveling in walking buses. Long lines of children, and several adults, walk around town collecting kids from each street. Walking to school is great exercise!

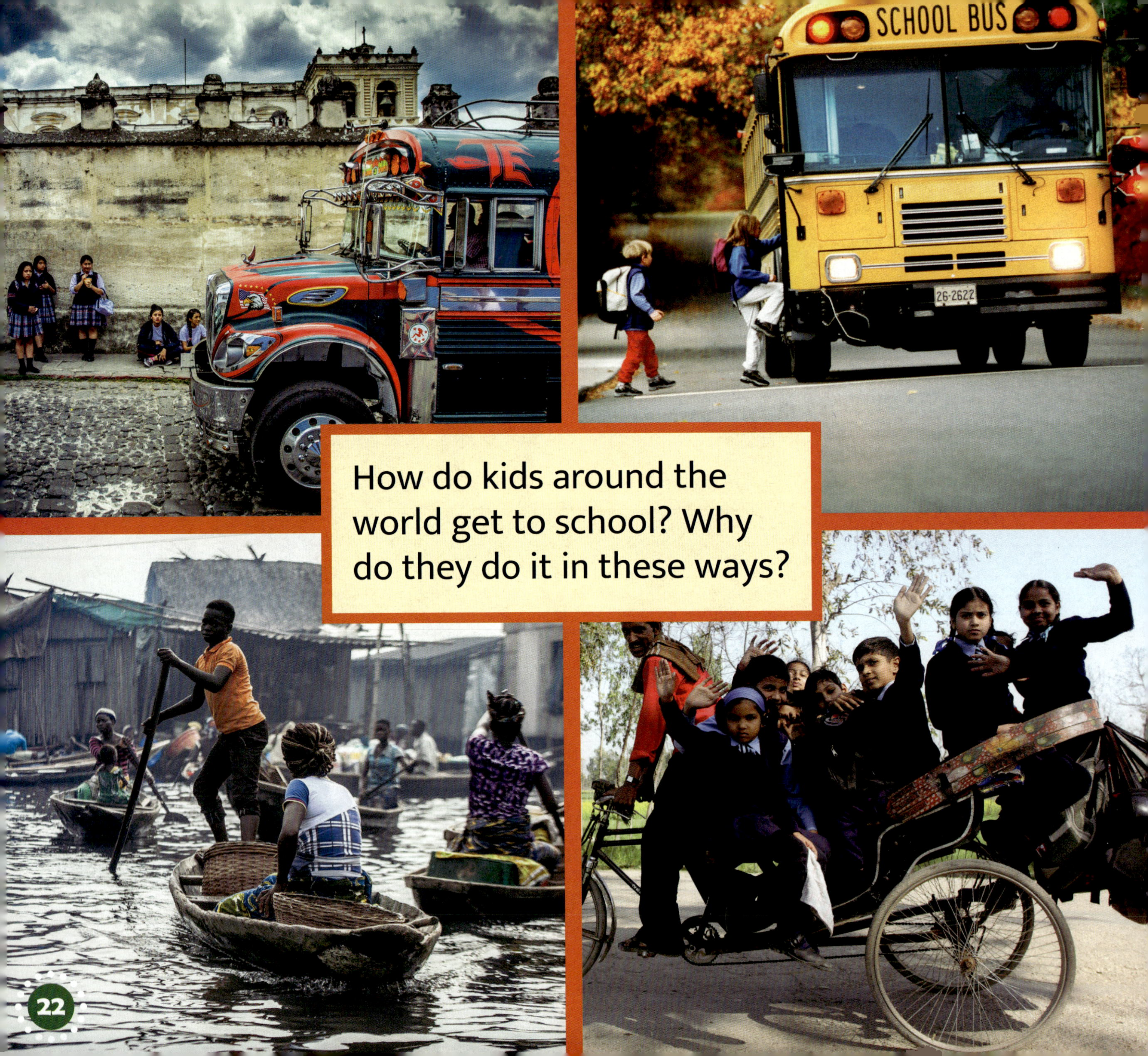

How do kids around the world get to school? Why do they do it in these ways?

What are some of the reasons why people go places?

KEY WORDS

Research has shown that as much as 65 percent of all written material published in English is made up of 300 words. These 300 words cannot be taught using pictures or learned by sounding them out. They must be recognized by sight. This book contains 117 common sight words to help young readers improve their reading fluency and comprehension. This book also teaches young readers several important content words, such as proper nouns. These words are paired with pictures to aid in learning and improve understanding.

Page	Sight Words First Appearance
4	a, and, are, around, be, by, can, cars, day, do, every, get, how, in, move, on, people, small, some, sometimes, the, these, they, we, when, will
5	from, home, is, looks, many, new, now, once, school, states, their, to, took, with
6	about, all, children, each, it, seen, takes, that
7	at, because, helps, keep, of, was
8	have, or, other, out
9	for, two
10	city, live, near, off, one, set, side, which, while
11	after, again, fathers, go, then, use
12	animal, our, over, them, time, were, years
13	its, miles, own, run
14	an, as, been, find, food, land, large, places, walk, world
15	call
16	way
17	almost, long, watch
18	always, come, if, it's, might, most, need, not, so
19	like
20	feet, there
21	great, lines
22	why
23	what

Page	Content Words First Appearance
4	cars, cities, Colombia, herders, Mongolia, motorbike, Myanmar, oxcarts, reindeer
5	bus, Guatemala, kids, paint, United States, village
6	Canada, drivers
7	Dearborn, Henry Ford Museum, Michigan
8	bicycle, carriages, Delhi, India, pedal, rickshaws, streets, vans
10	canoe, Lagos, lagoon, Nigeria
12	ancestors, camels, dogs, donkeys, horses
13	Greenland, ice, Inuit, owners, sled, snow
14	engine, Norway, Sami, snowmobiles
16	countries, holiday, train
17	Australia, China, maglev, screens, Shanghai
18	ambulance, doctors, emergency, hospital, outback, plane
19	patient
20	chairs, feet, South Africa
21	Great Britain, town

Published by Smartbook Media Inc.
350 5th Avenue, 59th Floor New York, NY 10118
Website: www.openlightbox.com

Printed in the United States of America in Brainerd, Minnesota
1 2 3 4 5 6 7 8 9 0 22 21 20 19 18

012018
120117

Library of Congress Cataloging in Publication Control Number: 2017959802

ISBN 978-1-5105-3540-4 (hardcover)
ISBN 978-1-5105-3541-1 (multi-user eBook)

Project Coordinator: John Willis
Art Director: Terry Paulhus

Every reasonable effort has been made to trace ownership and to obtain permission to reprint copyright material. The publisher would be pleased to have any errors or omissions brought to its attention so that they may be corrected in subsequent printings.
The publisher acknowledges Getty Images and Alamy as its primary image suppliers for this title.